# Field Animals

*written by Fae Hall    illustrated by John Roberts*

*Puffin Books*

Puffin Books: Penguin Books Ltd,
Harmondsworth, Middlesex, England
Penguin Books Inc.,
7110 Ambassador Road, Baltimore, Maryland 21207, U.S.A.
Penguin Books Australia Ltd,
Ringwood, Victoria, Australia
Penguin Books Canada Ltd,
41 Steelcase Road West, Markham, Ontario, Canada
Penguin Books (N.Z.) Ltd,
182–190 Wairau Road, Auckland 10, New Zealand

First published by Puffin Books 1975

Printed in Great Britain by
Colour Reproductions Ltd, Billericay, Essex, England

Fields are marvellous places for exploring,
and there are more animals in these fields
than you might imagine.

Rooks

**Rooks** and **crows** are large black birds.
**Rooks** have bare faces and 'baggy trousered' legs.
They make twig nests at the top of tall trees.
In spring you can see them carrying corn
and other food for their young in a special pouch
in their throats.  Rooks feed in large flocks.

**Crows** feed mainly in pairs or small groups.
They bury what food they don't need.
They eat eggs and young birds as well as seeds and plants.
At the seaside you sometimes see crows carrying crabs
or other shellfish.  They drop them from a height
to break the shell so they can eat the flesh inside.

Crows

5

A Highland cow

Once all **cows** looked rather like the shaggy
Highland cattle, and had long thin horns.  Now we have
many different kinds of cattle. They provide us
with meat and milk.  A dairy cow with a calf can give
up to 15 litres of milk each day for 10 or 11 months.
People have kept cows for more than 6,000 years.

*facing page : Top* Ayrshire, Red Poll, Belted Galloway, Guernsey
*Middle* A Guernsey and a British Friesian
*Bottom* Hereford cow and calf

The **magpie** is an easy bird to spot.
It has a long tail and black and white feathers.
Its twiggy nest is completely closed in
except for a hole on one side.  It is lined
with earth and fine roots, and is built in April
in a thick hedge or at the top of tall trees.
Magpies are famous for collecting
shiny and coloured objects.  No one knows why they do it.
Magpies eat almost anything, from corn and caterpillars,
to eggs, baby birds, and rabbits.

**Brown hares** live in the open
in the middle of large fields,
and like to feed on farm crops, especially turnips.
Usually you will see only one hare in a field,
but in spring they gather in groups for breeding.
Baby hares, called *leverets*, are born in the open
and can run almost from birth.

**Rabbits** are related to hares but they are smaller, and have a white tail, and live in burrows, often in a bank or hedgerow. Usually many rabbits live together, and their young are born underground, in a special nest lined with fur, which the mother pulls from her body. Rabbits are born without fur, but by the time they are 10 days old their coats are fully grown.

12

**Sheep** were first kept for their meat and wool
over 8,000 years ago. Because they have
such thick woolly coats, we think they first came
from cold countries. Even now, sheep can stay outside
all winter long, and the farmer waits
for warm weather before he shears the wool
to sell for spinning and weaving into cloth.

**Stoats** and **weasels** have long thin reddish bodies.
The **stoat** has a black tip to its tail, and is a fierce hunter.
It lives on rabbits and other animals
which it kills by biting the back of the neck.

The tiny **weasel** has a skull so small
that it will pass through an average-size wedding ring.
Weasels feed on small animals such as mice and voles
and also baby birds and eggs.

(*left*) Stoat

(*below*) Weasel

We keep **pigs** for the meat and fat they provide.
One large pig can give about 100 kilogrammes
of pork or bacon. When they are in the fields

pigs use their long snouts to grub up food
such as roots, acorns and insects.  Long ago
people used herds of pigs to dig up the ground
ready for planting seeds in spring.

A sow and her piglets

**Pheasants** first came from Asia
and they were brought to Britain
over a thousand years ago,
perhaps by the Romans.
They spend most of their time
on the ground and rarely fly
or perch in trees except at night.

In spring, the brightly coloured cock pheasant
courts the hen bird with a special running dance.
The hen lays up to 15 olive-brown eggs in a nesting hollow
scraped out under a bush.  When the brown chicks hatch
the hen bird feeds them on bits of plants and insects.

**Hedgehogs** come out
in the evening or at night
and feed on slugs, snails,
worms and insects. They move
quite fast on their long legs,
snorting and snuffling
as they go. A hedgehog
protects itself by rolling up
into a spiny ball.

Adult hedgehogs have 15 stiff spines on each square centimetre of their bodies. When the four or five baby hedgehogs are born in the leafy nest in the hedgerow their spines are pale and soft.

# Honey bees

Gardeners keep the small brown **honey bee** in hives
for the honey it stores to feed its young.
Until 200 years ago, honey was the only kind of sugar
which the people in Europe had.

In the summer, bees buzz in the fields and hedges
collecting nectar from the centre of one flower.
They carry away on their bodies the pollen
which the next flower will need to produce its seeds.
The large and loudly buzzing queen bumble bee
sleeps through the winter and appears at primrose time
searching for a hole in a bank in which to make her nest.

Queen bumble bee

**Worms** usually come out at night, so we do not see many.
It is hard to believe that one very small field
may contain over 100,000! They are useful to farmers
because they improve the condition of the soil.
Worms can move weights of up to 50 grammes
with their mouths. Look carefully at the ground in winter
and you will see where a worm has plugged
the opening of its burrow with leaves,
or a small pile of stones.

**Robins** are familiar birds in gardens and fields
as they fly from the hedge to the garden and back again,
picking up insects and worms.
The male and the female robin both have red breasts.
They puff them out when they sing their sweet song
as a warning to other robins
to keep away from their territory.
In spring, the hen bird stops singing
and builds a neat, hair-lined nest,
in which she lays five or six reddish speckled eggs.

If you see a field where there are fresh molehills
you may be lucky enough to see the earth moving
as a **mole** tunnels below the surface in search of worms.
    Usually all burrows in one part of a field
belong to one mole.  Every day a mole eats
more than half its weight in worms and insects.
Some moles make underground larders,
in which they store as many as 500 worms.
They use their extra broad hands for digging.
A mole will feel its way in the darkness underground
by the means of sensitive hairs on its head and tail.

common blue
(male)

painted lady
(male)

painted lady
(female)

wall brown
(male)

small tortoiseshell
(male)

meadow
brown
(male)

wall brown
(female)

caterpillar
of small
tortoiseshell

meadow
brown
(female)

peacock
(male)

small heath
(male)

peacock
(male)

30

chrysalis of
peacock

caterpillar of
peacock

clouded yellow
(male)

large white
(female)

orange tip
(male)

large white
(female)

marbled white
(male)

common
blue
(female)

small heath
(male)

marbled white
(female)

common blue
(male)

small copper
(male)

**Butterflies** are amongst the largest and most beautiful
of insects.  In Britain there are about 70 different kinds.
They prefer bright sunny days for flying.
Some of the butterflies we see in our fields fly to Britain
across the sea from Europe.  Butterflies feed on ripe fruits
and the nectar of flowers.  Look at one sideways
and you will see its long tongue coiled beneath its head.
A butterfly egg hatches into a **caterpillar**
which feeds on plants, and then turns into a **chrysalis**,
from which a new butterfly eventually comes.

**Partridges** are round, plump birds which live in fields, but their brown speckled plumage makes them difficult to see.  They often move in families and feed on flowers and green plants.  They enjoy a dust bath to clean their feathers when the weather is dry. Each hen partridge lays up to 20 eggs, which all hatch at once. The tiny chicks can run almost from the time they hatch.

You can find more animals in the fields. Remember – just stand and watch.